FOREWORD BY KENDA CREASY DEAN

RAISING TEENS IN AN ALMOST CHRISTIAN WORLD

A PARENT'S GUIDE

BY DIETRICH KIRK

⚬cymt

CYMT Press

Raising Teens in an Almost Christian World: A Parents Guide
©2012 by Dietrich Kirk

CYMT Press is an imprint of the Center for Youth Ministry Training; 309 Franklin Road, Brentwood, Tennessee 37027.

ISBN-13 978-1-937734-02-2

Web site addresses listed in this book were current at the time of publication. Please contact Center for Youth Ministry Training via e-mail (Info@CYMT.org) to report URLs that are no longer operational and replacement URLs if available.

Editorial direction by Tim Baker
Art direction by David Conn
Line editing by Julia Canada Wilburn

Printed in the United States

C●NTENTS

ACKNOWLEDGEMENTS

This resource is the result of a conversation with Chris Coble at the Lilly Foundation. I am grateful to the Lilly Foundation for its investment in youth ministry training through the Center for Youth Ministry Training (CYMT) and its trust in CYMT to translate their research into actionable tools. Our hope is that *Raising Teens in Almost Christian World: A Parent's Guide* is the first in a series of resources that not only translate the research of the National Study on Youth and Religion, but also bring transformation to churches, families, and the lives of young people.

I am grateful to the following groups of people for their impact on this project:

Kenda Creasy Dean is leading the way in challenging the church to think theologically about what it means to minister to and with youth. She is a great friend who challenges and inspires me. Kenda did the hard work of thinking theologically and practically to develop *Almost Christian*, her response to the National Study on Youth and Religion. I feel blessed to come alongside her brilliant work and provide practical insights for parents.

Andrew Zirschky originally wrote the introduction as a "nutshell summary" of *Almost Christian* as an article for YMToday.com. It is quite useful in this context to provide an overview of Dean's response to the National Study of Youth and Religion.

God has blessed the CYMT with an amazing board who faithfully serve so others may be blessed. Mark DeVries, our chair, is a teacher, mentor, and friend. CYMT's staff (Lesleigh, Julia, Andrew, Mindi, Keeley, and Jim) are ministry partners who faithfully seek to serve God by equipping and empowering youth ministers to reach this generation for Christ.

Brentwood United Methodist Church, Northside United Methodist Church, Aldersgate United Methodist Church, and Trinity United Methodist Church for nurturing a young youth minister and showing him God's grace as we journeyed together.

My parents for having behind-the-wall conversations, presenting disorienting dilemmas, creating Godly traditions, and making God a part of our family experience. My brother, Andrew, who serves God with all his heart.

My wife and love of my life, Keeley, who is my companion on this life journey as we seek to introduce our daughters to Christ so that they might experience the life giving grace we have received.

Parents of youth in my program who reminded me over the years that I would be a better youth minister when I had kids. You were right!

FOREWORD

Kenda Creasy Dean

When my kids were small, the brutal murder of a family two doors down caused us to seek out a family counselor. We knew that Shannon, our two-year-old, wouldn't remember it, but we were concerned about the event's effects on Brendan, who was six. After several weeks of getting to know us, the counselor gave us her advice. I remember being nervous as we entered her office, bracing myself to hear all the ways I was already messing up my son with my best efforts at being a mother.

The counselor didn't criticize us; instead, she gave us some strategies for helping Brendan deal with anxiety. She advised us to let him work out his fears through play. "Don't sweat the action figures" she said, looking directly at me. "Play between 'good guys and bad guys' is one way children come to terms with the fact that evil exists in the world but it doesn't have to win. Playing Power Rangers won't turn him into an ax murderer. It helps him feel like he has some mastery over a dangerous world when he joins the Red and Green Rangers in defeating Lord Zedd." Keep up the karate lessons, she told us, and continue making home a safe and loving place. When he gets anxious, take it seriously.

"Oh, and one more thing," she said gently, knowing that I was a pastor. "You'll have to think about this, but you might consider laying off the religion."

What is a pastor supposed to do when a family counselor's advice for a child is to "lay off the religion"? Kevin and I were intentionally trying to raise our children as Christians, and we knew that transformative faith in Jesus Christ does not happen by osmosis. We did what most Christian parents do: we read our kids Bible stories, prayed with them, involved them in choir and Sunday school and worship. We made sure they understood the religious meaning of holidays, and both our kids learned that, if you want to stay up past bedtime, engage Mom in a religious discussion. She'll forget all about what time it is. Was this detrimental to our children? What does "laying off the religion" look like when you desperately want your children to have the best source of joy in life that you know: life-giving, liberating, self-giving faith in Jesus Christ?

At first, I was deeply offended by the counselor's advice, thinking she was suggesting that we were harming our children by raising them as Christians. After all, religious people have committed horrific crimes while hiding under Christianity's vestments. From the crusades to genocide to a summer camp in Norway, the ease with which humans use religion to justify violence illustrates how easily religious ideologies can be manipulated for diabolical ends. The father who murdered his family in our neighborhood on that awful night had ended the killing spree by dismantling the fire alarms, setting the neighborhood on fire, and committing suicide on a bed beside an open Bible.

It is common for us to understand Christianity merely as a set of religious ideals, not a life-giving identity. We Christian parents would probably say we trust Jesus, but our lives often tell a different story. Look at our overscheduled calendars, our insatiable consumerism, our relentless anxiety as a culture… we're as vulnerable to these idols as anybody else. Our kids know us for who we really are. One glance at our lives tells the truth.

The most incontrovertible finding of the National Study of Youth and Religion (2004) is that "we get what we are" with our children, in religion as in most things.[1] Faith is a gift from God, not an ideology we can instill; getting kids to believe "in" Jesus is fine, but in the end, it doesn't change very much. *Trusting* Jesus, on the other hand—*believing* Jesus, having confidence in God's forgiveness and redemption and that Christ has made the future a good and promising place to go—is a different way to live. Trust changes things. Trust quells anxiety. Trust inspires hope. Trust alters how we live, allowing us to live on God's timeline instead of ours. If youth are to discover faith in Jesus Christ through us, they are going to need to see us live out our trust in Him.

Of course, preparing a six-year-old for Christian faith includes telling him the stories of faith and inviting him to participate in the broader Christian community as well. But these are secondary. What Brendan really wanted at age six—and at age 16, and at every age we confront a sinful, inexplicable world—was a God who could dispel anxiety instead of contribute to it. He needed to see his parents *living* the Bible stories we read at bedtime to interpret our family's experience of the world, and to see us turn to the church community to discern God's movement amid the chaos of everyday life. Above all, he needed to watch how, in good times and in bad, his parents *trusted* God with our futures, and with his.

Lives lived in this reassurance are different than those drenched in anxiety. So it may be that the very best thing that could happen to Christian parenting is that we "lay off the religion"—which means, of course, that we must attend to *faith*, a life bound to Christ in hope, trust, and love. You are doing that by using this parents' guide, and by wrestling with what it means to raise young people with consequential Christian faith. The fact that you are doing this with other parents is significant; Christianity, like raising children, is a shared endeavor. You will find in the pages that follow handy summaries, provocative discussion starters, and a good deal of soul searching as we learn together ways to approach young people more faithfully.

I wish I could say that we did everything right as we tried to raise our children in Christian faith. We didn't (and our kids will be the first to tell you that). But we didn't do everything wrong, either—and neither will you. The fact is that grace covers a multitude of sins, including the ones parents visit on their children. In the end, our children belong to God, not to us, which means their faith is in God's hands, not ours. Our job is to help our children recognize the gift of faith that God has given to them, and to offer ample opportunities for living it out.

Your very interest in this study means you are already tackling some of the issues it raises, and your children are already reaping the benefits of having parents who invest in their own faith. Your children notice the way you live, and your faith is giving them hope. May the next few weeks bathe you in grace, and help you "lay off the religion" in favor of loving Christ.

Kenda Creasy Dean
Princeton Theological Seminary
July 25, 2011

INTRODUCTION
Becoming Christian-*ish*: Research in a Nutshell

"We have come with some confidence to believe that a significant part of Christianity in the United States is actually only tenuously Christian in any sense that it is seriously connected to the actual historical Christian tradition... It is not so much that U.S. Christianity is being secularized. Rather, more subtly, Christianity is either degenerating into a pathetic version of itself or, more significantly, Christianity is actively being colonized and displaced by quite a different religious faith."[1]

–Christian Smith and Melinda Denton,
from the National Study for Youth and Religion

SETTING THE STAGE:

The National Study on Youth and Religion (NSYR) reported that a majority of American teenagers described themselves as Christian, but in reality they espouse a version of Christianity the researchers termed "Moralistic Therapeutic Deism." Kenda Creasy Dean was one of the study's researchers. *Almost Christian* is response to how the church should move forward in light of the findings. This study guide will explore the findings of the National Study on Youth and Religion and use Dean's work in *Almost Christian* to reflect on how we can respond to this study.

THE NATIONAL STUDY ON YOUTH & RELIGION:

Since 2001, a team of researchers headed by sociologist Christian Smith (University of Notre Dame) has been studying the spiritual lives of American adolescents in what is arguably the largest study ever conducted around youth and religion. The study has produced numerous articles and reports (available at youthandreligion.org) and in addition, two books summarizing the find-ings. Soul Searching, released in 2005, details findings from an initial phone survey of 3,000 young people and their parents, along with data collected through extensive face-to-face interviews with a subset of study participants.

In 2009 Smith released a second book, *Souls in Transition*, which documents follow-up research on the same group of young people as they have entered college and the workforce. The overall goal of the project is to investigate both the influence of religion on American teenagers and the practices that religious communities employ for the spiritual formation of young people.

This landmark study on the faith lives of American teenagers reveals that while a majority identifies with a religious congregation, many adolescents:

1. Lack the ability to speak articulately about their faith;
2. Believe that religion itself is not terribly important to daily life; and
3. Subscribe to a watered-down belief system that the authors call Moralistic Therapeutic Deism.

The study attempts to take stock of what American teenagers really believe and how they practice their faith while assessing the influence of parents, peers, churches, and other factors upon adolescent faith. For Christian youth ministry, the study may reveal ways in which current attempts at forming adolescent faith are either succeeding or failing miserably.

MAJOR FINDINGS

The study uncovered numerous findings about the faith of the American teen-ager, such as socio-economic influences and geographical factors. Those influ-ences, while important, are outside the scope of this project. Generally, the study revealed seven major findings that have direct importance for youth ministry.

1. Most American teenagers have religious beliefs.

Current studies on the faith of the American teenager often report that stu-dents are hostile toward religion. Smith's report actually points us in a dif-ferent direction. He reports that roughly two-thirds of American teenagers believe in a god who is similar to the God of the Bible.[2] More than 84 percent of teenagers identify themselves as religious, and the vast majority of them (75 percent) claims to be Christian.[3] Half of American teenagers report that religion is "very important" or "extremely important" to them.[4] Forty per-cent of teenagers attend religious services weekly or more often.

2. Organized religion doesn't matter much to most teenagers.

The NSYR reveals that teenagers have inconsequential feelings about religion which means it doesn't make a difference in their everyday lives. For most teenagers, religion is a "very nice thing," but not something they care much about. Teenagers do not look to religion to frame their identities. Religion is unimportant to them. This apathy led Smith to describe the dominant teenage attitude toward Christianity as "benign whateverism." A majority of teenagers report that they have close friends with whom they have never discussed religion.

3. For a significant minority of teenagers, faith does matter.

While benign whateverism is rampant, Smith identifies a minority of teenagers as "highly devoted." Faith is a guiding force for this subset of students. These teenagers are more likely to be evangelical or Mormon than mainline or Catholic. They are more likely to have married, highly educated parents who also attend religious services often. They are more likely to be girls than boys, and more likely to be younger teenagers than older. They are more likely to be involved in a youth group, and to have close friends involved in a religious group. For these teens faith is consequential; it matters in their everyday life.

4. Adolescents are incredibly inarticulate about their faith.

The NSYR found that teenagers suffer from an impoverished ability to talk about their faith, possibly because they are rarely encouraged to critically think through their faith. Even those who reported that religion was important to them were often woefully unable to express what they believe or why their beliefs are important to them. The study found that youth were very articulate about other subjects. Smith suggests that this religious inarticulacy is due to churches "failing rather badly in religiously engaging and educating youth."[5]

5. Religious vitality differs by tradition.

Mormon youth ranked incredibly high in their ability to articulate their faith, and the effects their faith has on their lives. Conservative Protestants came in second along with Black Protestant teenagers. Religious vitality among mainline Protestant and Roman Catholic teenagers was lower.

6. Highly religious teenagers fare better than less religious teenagers.

In terms of a variety of life outcomes, Smith found that highly religious teenagers are doing better across the board than their less religious peers. Whether they realize it or not, more religious teenagers fare better than less religious teenagers in terms of "risk behaviors, quality of family and adult relationships, moral reasoning and behavior, community participation, media consumption, sexual activity, and emotional well-being."[6]

7. Teenagers mimic the religious devotion of their parents.

The NSYR found that parents are the greatest influence on teenage faith. Teenagers tend to share beliefs similar to their parents, subscribe to the same religious tradition, and attend religious services with a similar frequency.[7] This is good news, but also deeply troubling in light of the invasion of what Smith terms "Moralistic Therapeutic Deism" into the American religious landscape.

ALMOST CHRISTIAN: A PRACTICAL RESPONSE

Kenda Creasy Dean is an ordained United Methodist pastor in the Baltimore-Washington Annual Conference and Professor of Youth, Church and Culture at Princeton Theological Seminary, where she works closely with the Institute for Youth Ministry.

Dean names the self-centered faith found by the NSYR with the simple term, "*Almost* Christian." Dean's 2010 book (by this same title) explores how the church and parents can respond to the findings.

Advocating ways to develop consequential faith in American teenagers is the main thrust of *Almost Christian*. The book is an attempt to address the NSYR's research by examining what the church and parents can learn from the small percentage of "highly devoted" students found in the study. Dean weaves together sociological theory along with empirical research on the faith lives of adolescents from the ongoing National Study of Youth and Religion to give readers an understanding of four common traits of teenagers who possess consequential faith.

After identifying the characteristics of teenagers with consequential faith, Dean addresses how we go about nurturing those characteristics in youth. For that task, she jumps from sociology into a deep exploration of Christian theology to highlight three historic Christian "arts" (or practices) that hold promise for building a "framework" upon which consequential faith can grow. As a Christian theologian, Dean is quick to recognize faith as the unique gift of the Holy Spirit, but she also emphasizes that parents and faith communities play an integral role in preparing young people for faith that matters.

Dean is interested in exploring what allows some teenagers to have a faith that makes a difference in their lives, and what causes other teenagers to practice Christianity with "benign whateverism"—a positive disposition toward Christianity, but one that makes little change in their lives.

HOW TO USE THIS BOOK

This resource contains the following six lessons, designed to inform parents, to prompt reflection, and to provide tangible next steps. In this study you'll learn more about these six key areas:

1. Benign Whateverism
2. Faith that Bears Fruit
3. Passing on the Faith
4. Testify by Word and Action
5. Transformation through Disorientation
6. Hope for Tomorrow

Each lesson contains the following sections to help guide you as you reflect on how the session impacts your students and your family. If you are leading a group that is doing this study together, remember to prepare in advance, making sure that you understand the focus of each lesson and have all of the necessary tools pulled together.

- **Setting the Stage** – A brief introduction to the topic.
- **From the Study** – A look at findings from the National Study on Youth and Religion that relate to the topic.
- **Looking at Scripture** – A scriptural reflection that theologically informs each topic.
- **Dean's Response** – A summary of Dean's response to this finding.
- **Exploring Our Response** – An opportunity to reflect and begin to form our own conclusions.
- **Discussion Questions** – Questions intended for each parent or couple to reflect on together.

Each lesson is followed by four resources to help parents address each week's topic in their families in a variety of ways:

- **Conversation Starters** – A place to begin as you seek to engage your youth in dialogue on each topic.
- **Tradition Builders** – Ideas for how you might build traditions in your family that inform your children's understanding of who God is.
- **Disorienting Dilemmas** – Ways of creating space for the Holy Spirit to work by expanding your youth's understanding.
- **Experiencing Together** – Activities you can do together as a family that provide opportunities for hands on learning, modeling the faith, and follow up conversation.

The National Study on Youth and Religion has shown us that the church and parents are having a difficult time passing on the Christian faith to young people. The God they have come to believe in is far removed from the God who gives all to be with us and live within us. We pray this study will encourage you on your journey as a family to know and love God. May the Holy Spirit divinely empower your efforts so that your children may come to live for Christ!

Lesson One
BENIGN WHATEVERISM

That which dominates our imaginations and our
thoughts will determine our lives, and our character.
Therefore, it behooves us to be careful what we worship,
for what we are we are worshipping we are becoming.

—*Ralph Waldo Emerson*[1]

SETTING THE STAGE:

In this lesson we will explore benign whateverism and the guiding belief of
Moralistic Therapeutic Deism. We will discuss both of these cultural trends,
and evaluate whether they are present in our churches and homes.

FROM THE STUDY:

According to Smith and Denton, "Teenagers tend to view God as either a
cosmic butler or a divine therapist, someone who meets their needs when
summoned or who listens nonjudgmentally and helps them feel good about
themselves. Teenagers are not hostile toward religion: they just do not care
about it very much. Religion is not a big deal to them. People fight over things
that matter to them—but religion barely causes a ripple in the lives of most
adolescents. Butlers and lifeguards watch from the sidelines until called upon;
therapists and guidance counselors offer encouragement and advice."[2]

While Benign Whateverism might not seem like a big deal (after all,
haven't all of us unleashed a snarky "whatever!" to our parents?), according to
the NSYR, Benign Whateverism is a symptom to a deeper current Smith and
Denton identify as "Moralistic Therapeutic Deism." Many scholars point to
the idea of MTD as the most accurate description of student culture.

GUIDING BELIEFS OF MORALISTIC THERAPEUTIC DEISM

1. A God exists who created and orders the world and watches over life on earth.
2. God wants people to be good, nice, and fair to each other, as taught in the Bible and by most world religions.
3. The central goal of life is to be happy and to feel good about oneself.
4. God is not involved in my life except when I need God to resolve a problem.
5. Good people go to heaven when they die.[3]

DEAN'S RESPONSE:

In *Almost Christian*, Dean unpacks the following key concepts within Moralistic Therapeutic Deism that are counter to the Christian worldview.

Choose four adults in the group and ask each one to read aloud one of the following points.

1. MTD reduces Christian ethics to being nice. Jesus never specifically asks believers to be nice. Instead, the gospel invites believers to be kind, compassionate, do justice, live forgiveness, love their enemies. Those are a lot harder than just being nice!

The result is that biblical ethics are reduced to a set of moral beliefs that have no teeth. Moral truths found in scripture are translated into the life of the student as "suggestions for life." Ethics become suggestions one can adopt or reject, with little influence on the life of the believer. In short, the truth of the Ten Commandments and the importance of the teachings of Jesus are stripped of their importance and reduced to a common list of rules one *ought* to follow if they want to be happy.

2. MTD is all about individual comfort and happiness. Moralistic Therapeutic Deism leads students to believe that God exists to meet their needs and help them be nice people who feel good about themselves. God exists to make people happy and successful.

Scripture teaches us that God wants us to be happy, but that personal self-fulfillment is not the source of genuine happiness. True joy comes from sharing our humanity with others—our delights and our suffering.

Sharing our lives means that when our neighbor suffers, we are called to step in and help carry one another's burdens.

3. *MTD cannot withstand life's challenges.* What happens when a believer's life falls apart? What happens when the believer hits rock bottom? If religion exists for the purpose of "feeling good" and "doing nice things," life's challenges render religion irrelevant. Religion does not help an abuse victim "feel good" about the abuse she suffered, nor does it help her "be nice" to her abuser (nor should it).

This contrasts with the Christian belief system. Believers are called to take up their cross, which is a clear call toward suffering. When Christian communities embody the crucified-death-resurrection example found in the life of Jesus, the church participates in God's process of transformation that leads to "new birth." Through his life, death, and resurrection, Christ does not merely glue our shattered selves back together; he makes us brand new.

4. *MTD offers a fragile framework for hope.* Millennial young people believe that their decisions are mostly made for them, and they have little influence in the world. Why should we care about having influence if those around us are making decisions that make us happy? But when MTD-ists encounter despair; decisions are being made that victimize us, and there's nothing we can do about it. In the theological world of MTD, hope goes down the drain at this point. Where is this God who is supposed to make me so happy?

The gospels teach that our lives and our futures belong to God, but at the same time, God calls us to participate in God's movement through history. In other words, God could work alone, but chooses not to—and in fact, God calls each of us to participate in moving the world toward the mission of God. God's gift to us is hope: a trust that, despite present problems, the world is going in a good direction—and that we participate in getting it there.[4]

LOOKING AT SCRIPTURE: MATTHEW 7:7-12

Spend some time reading this passage together. Keep in mind the guiding principles of MTD as you read.

"Ask and it will be given to you; seek and you will find; knock and the door will be opened to you. For everyone who asks receives; the one who seeks finds; and to the one who knocks, the door will be opened.

"Which of you, if your son asks for bread, will give him a stone? Or if he asks for a fish, will give him a snake? If you, then, though you are evil, know how to give good gifts to your children, how much more will your Father in heaven give good gifts to those who ask him! So in everything, do to others what you would have them do to you, for this sums up the Law and the Prophets." Matthew 7:7-12, NIV

After you've read the passage above, reflect on these questions:

- What would Moralistic Therapeutic Deists take away from this passage?
- Does this passage support the guiding beliefs of Moralistic Therapeutic Deism?
- Is this scripture a complete picture of the Gospel? How does it support Moralistic Therapeutic Deism?
- What scriptures come to mind that speak to MTD?

EXPLORING OUR RESPONSE:

Dean points out that "Moralistic Therapeutic Deism offers comfort, bolsters, self-esteem, helps solve problems, and lubricates interpersonal relationships by encouraging people to do good, feel good, and keep God at arm's length. It is a self-emolliating spirituality; its thrust is personal happiness and helping people treat each other nicely."[5]

This belief system is a far cry for the sacrificial life-giving faith that historic Christianity claims. The fact is that MTD exists in your home. So the prevailing question is this: how should parents respond to MTD? What practical solutions do we have for Benign Whateverism?

DISCUSSION QUESTIONS:

Spend a few minutes as a group reacting to the following questions:

- In light of the National Study of Youth and Religion's finding, Dean states that most teenagers think of God as either "a divine therapist" or "a cosmic butler."

> – Is this shift present in your church? Where?
> – How have you seen this shift in the teenagers you know?
> – Where have you seen this shift in your student?

- Read the "Guiding Beliefs of Moralistic Therapeutic Deism" in the shaded box on page 20. Now say the Apostles' Creed. What are the differences? What do they tell us?
- Does the National Study of Youth and Religion reflect the youth in your congregation?
- If the study profiled the adults in your congregation, would they have found different results?
- The study showed that teenagers' response to religion was best described as "benign whateverism." Religion just isn't a big deal to them. Are the teenagers in your church and home passionate about anything? Where are they placing their energy and passion? Why?

WORDS OF ASSURANCE

"Everything you need for your children's faith formation, God had already given you. Awakening faith does not depend on how hard we press young people to love God, but on how much we show them that we do."[6] —Dean

Lesson One
FAITH TOOLS

Moralistic Therapeutic Deism comes with opportunities. Parents who desire for their families to grow closer to the Lord will recognize MTD's opportunities for deep faith conversations. The following exercises will plunge your family into moments where you have the opportunity to unpack the beliefs of your children, and to express your own understanding of who God is.

CONVERSATION STARTERS:

Who is God?

One of the ways to get faith conversations going is to ask questions. Questions ignite discussions and give you a chance to explain your faith journey to your student. Questions also give students opportunities to express their own faith, and their doubt as well. When we engage students in faith conversations through questions, we should be prepared for a variety of potential topics. If you ask a child or youth a question, then you should be prepared to receive a question in return. If you do, you have started a conversation. Consider exploring the following questions with your students sometime this week. You might want to bring up a question while you're on the way to school or to the store. Or, consider bringing up one of these questions after dinner.

- Do you know why I believe in God? Jesus?
- What do you believe about God? Jesus?
- Where have you seen God today? Or this week?

If those questions don't feel like a correct fit for the kind of faith conversation you want to have with your student, consider asking him a question that you haven't answered. Ask him about one of God's character traits that you don't understand, or invite him to discuss a theological concept. When you ask the question, allow your student time to respond to the question. Don't try to correct her thinking by telling her she is wrong, as that will close off the conversation. Instead, teach her by sharing what you believe.

TRADITION BUILDER:

Worship

The most common tradition Christians have is attending church, but we don't all worship in the same way. Have you ever talked with your family about *why* you attend worship? Do your students know why you're members at your church? Do you worship together or does everyone sit in different places in the sanctuary, or in different rooms within the church? It's important to engage our students in conversations about worship. Talk as a family about what worship should be. Use these questions to explore what worship could become in your family.

- Why do you think we go to church?
- What is the purpose of worship?
- What parts of the worship service do you like? Not like? Have questions about?
- How can we help each other worship more fully?

DISORIENTING DILEMMAS

How does your student perceive the importance of faith in his or her life? Asking directly can be tricky, and might cause him to close in, and not talk about his faith. Instead of talking to her about her faith, consider asking about a friend's faith. Look for an opportunity to ask something like, "Is faith important to your friends?" Follow up with, "How can you tell?"

If your student is open to the conversation, follow up with other questions about students outside their circles of friends. Consider asking, "Who in your school lives their faith?" and "What do the Christian kids at your school talk about?"

Because the NSYR affirms that youth rarely talk about their faith, you may create a disorienting dilemma for them simply by engaging them in this kind of conversation. And, it's important to remember that engaging your student in faith conversations should be pursued gently, with a spirit of openness and with a non judgmental attitude.

EXPERIENCING TOGETHER

Find a Saint

An excellent way of challenging the faith of your student is to offer them a "Senior Saint" they can interact with and look up to. Who does your family know that is a living "heirloom" of the faith? Who would you like to expose your children or youth to?

Make plans as a family to visit one of those people or have them over for dinner. Let them know in advance that you'd like for them to share some of their faith stories with your children. As you visit with them, open the door for them to share by simply saying something like:

- "You have been a member of our church for a long time. What does that mean to you?
- How has your relationship with Christ changed your life?
- Have you ever doubted your faith? Tell us about that.
- What do you love about Christ?

Saints are full of stories. Once the door is open, they will share, and their stories will shape your teen. Young people are fascinated by the testimonies of folks who live what they believe. They will listen and learn.

Lesson Two
FAITH THAT BEARS FRUIT

*Teenagers with every apparent religious advantage
remain practically numb to God's presence in their lives.
Why?*[1]

—Kenda Creasy Dean

SETTING THE STAGE:

A creed is a set of beliefs on which the church agrees. It's a set of faith statements organized into a statement of faith. In this lesson we'll learn what a creed is, why it's so important for the family, and for creating "fully devoted teenagers." We'll also learn how claiming a particular God story is essential to developing faith that bears fruit.

FROM THE STUDY:

What contributes to consequential faith? How does a teenager's faith shape the way they live? While the NSYR found that a sizeable number of teenagers attend church, just 8 percent could be classified as "highly devoted" teenagers whose faith makes a significant difference in their actions, identities, and lives. The chart on the following page helps illustrate that idea.

Four Religion Ideal Types in the National Study of Youth and Religion [2]	
THE DEVOTED 8% of American Youth	• Attends religious services weekly or more • Faith is very or extremely important in everyday life • Feels very or extremely close to God • Prays a few times a week or more • Reads scripture once or twice a week or more
THE REGULAR 27% of American Youth	• Attends religious services 2-3 times a month or weekly • Faith is very or somewhat important in everyday life • Closeness to God, youth group involvement, prayer, and scripture reading are variable but less religious than for the "devoted."
THE SPORADIC 17% of American Youth	• Attends religious services a few times a month to monthly • Faith is somewhat to not very important in everyday life • Closeness to God, youth group involvement, prayer, and scripture reading are variable
THE DISENGAGED 12% of American Youth	• Never attends religious services, or attends many times a year and identifies as not religious • Faith is somewhat, now very, or not important in everyday life • Feels only somewhat close to God or less • Not involved in a religious youth group • Prays 1-2 times a month or less

What are the characteristics of a "highly devoted" student? The NSYR discovered that "highly devoted" teens had the following characteristics in common. These students:

- Claimed a Creed
- Belonged to a Community
- Pursued a Calling
- Harbored Hope

Another study identified similar characteristics. The Exemplary Youth Ministry study, funded by The Lilly Foundation, looked at congregations that were forming transformational faith in young people and analyzed what they had in common. The churches selected were denominationally and racially diverse. Among the study's findings, they developed a list of characteristics found in mature Christian youth. They discovered that students from these congregations:

1. *Seek spiritual growth, both alone and with others.* They pursue questions, guidance, and commitment through conversation, study, Bible reading, prayer, small groups, retreats, etc.

2. *Are keenly aware of God.* They view God as active and present in their own life, in the lives of others, and in the life of the world.

3. *Act out of a commitment to faith in Jesus Christ.* They act privately and publicly, through regular worship, participation in ministry, and leadership in a congregation.

4. *Make Christian faith a way of life.* How? By recognizing God's "call" and integrating their beliefs into conversation, decisions, and actions in daily life.

5. *Live lives of service by being involved in caring for others and addressing injustice and immorality.*

6. *Reach out to others who are different or in need through prayer, hospitality, conversation, and support.*

7. *Exercise moral responsibility by living with integrity and utilizing faith in making considered moral decisions.*

8. *Speak publicly about faith by speaking openly about Jesus Christ and God's participation in their own lives and in the world.*

9. *Possess a positive, hopeful spirit towards others and life.*[3]

DEAN'S RESPONSE:

In pinpointing the struggle many teens face today, Dean describes the journey students are on toward claiming a creed. Choose one adult to read the following excerpt from *Almost Christian* aloud to the group.

Even if teenagers immerse themselves in youth ministry programs, are involved in churches, and manage to dodge overwhelming counterinfluences, they are unlikely to take hold of a "god" who is too limp to take hold of them. Perhaps young people lack robust Christian identities because churches offer such a stripped-down version of Christianity that it no longer poses a viable alternative to imposter spiritualties like Moralistic Therapeutic Deism. If teenagers lack an articulate faith, maybe it is because the faith we show them is too spineless to merit much in the way of conversation. Maybe teenagers' inability to talk about religion is not because the church inspires a faith too deep for words, but because the God-story that we tell is too vapid to merit more than a superficial vocabulary.

The elephant in the room in the discussion about the National Study of Youth and Religion is the muddled ecclesiology of American churches, a confusion present, not only in young people but in congregations themselves. We have forgotten that we are not here for ourselves, which has allowed self-focused spiritualties to put down roots in our soil. [4]

It would be unlikely for teenagers to develop any religious framework besides superficial Christianity if churches have supplanted the gospel with a religious outlook that functions primarily as a social lubricant, with a "god" who supports teenagers' decisions, makes them feel good about themselves, meets their needs when called upon but otherwise stays out of the way. If this is the god we offer young people, there may be little in Christianity to which they object, but there is even less to which they will be devoted. By contrast, the God portrayed in both the Hebrew and Christian Scriptures asks, not just for commitment, but for our very lives. The God of the Bible traffics in life and death, not niceness, and calls for sacrificial love, not benign whatever-ism. If the God of Jesus Christ is a missionary God who crosses every boundary—life and death and space and time—to win us, then following Jesus is bound to be anything but convenient.

The most likely explanation for Moralistic Therapeutic Deism is simply that we reap what we sow. We have received from teenagers exactly what we have asked them for: assent, not conviction; compliance, not faith. Young people invest in religion precisely what they think it is worth—and if they think the church is worthy of benign whatever-ism and no more, then the indictment falls not on them, but on us. [5]

Invite participants to reflect on Dean's words:

- Do you feel that Dean effectively summarizes the struggle your student faces?
- What elements within your home are working to create your student into a "highly devoted teen"?
- Consider Dean's warnings above. What statement might you take on as a challenge you want to try and meet within your home?

The God of Jesus Christ is a personal God who is active and involved in our lives. Dean points out that "highly devoted Christian teenagers espouse creeds that are unabashedly personal. They describe God as being personally concerned *for* them and powerfully involved *with* them—a stance precisely opposite that of classical deism."[6]

Many churches and families seem to have lost touch with how to pass on the faith. "We spend a lot of time hunting for gadgets, curriculum, methods, and even cultural tools that we hope will somehow convert human practices into holy fire. As long as we use the proper tools in the proper way with the proper timing, we tell ourselves, we can convert parental determination and pastoral energy into electrifying faith for the young people we love." Dean goes on to say, "The delusion that human effort can generate mature faith—in young people or anybody else—is as old as fiction itself." God alone can generate faith through the Holy Spirit, but we can be tools.[7]

Dean also notes that, "Witnessing to Christ presents a rather stark contrast to Christian attempts to dump Jesus onto people or to hand him over (as though he is ours to give) like a family heirloom that has historical or sentimental significance but is otherwise inert."[8]

LOOKING AT SCRIPTURE: MARK 12:28-31

In the following scripture, Jesus is approached by a teacher of the law, one who is clearly trying to catch Jesus in a trap. The Jews observed hundreds of laws, and it would be impossible for Jesus to choose one commandment as the most important. Jesus' choice not only stops the questioning from this teacher, it offers us a description of what a mature Christian looks like. Choose one adult in the group to read this passage aloud.

One of the teachers of the law came and heard them debating. Noticing that Jesus had given them a good answer, he asked him, "Of all the commandments, which is the most important?"

"The most important one," answered Jesus, "is this: 'Hear, O Israel: The Lord our God, the Lord is one. Love the Lord your God with all your heart and with all your soul and with all your mind and with all your strength.' The second is this: 'Love your neighbor as yourself.' There is no commandment greater than these." Mark 12:28-31, NIV

How do we know that we're connected to Christ and to the Christian community? Reflect on the following questions:

- What are the characteristics of a mature believer?
- How are you living out the idea of love in your life? In your family?
- How might this scripture help your family focus your life on God?

- What changes need to be made in the life of your church for your congregation to be known as "people who live love" in your community?

EXPLORING OUR RESPONSE:

One of the chief roles of the family is to claim "a particular God story." Dean suggests that one of our roles is to be the chief bards invoking our unique God story.

The National Study of Youth and Religion concluded that the best way for youth to become more serious about religious faith is for parents to become more serious about theirs. Parent religiosity during the teenage years was an even stronger predictor of young people's faith in emerging adulthood. Research is nearly unanimous on this point: parents matter most in shaping the religious lives of their children.

Do your children know why you go to church? Do they know your story and how Jesus changed your life? Is going to church changing your life? How is faith bearing fruit in your life? As the number one influencer on your child's faith, they need to *know* these things.

A family's traditions and rituals define who they are. If faith is not a part of these traditions, then we should not expect to have children with consequential faith! How does faith shape your family? How do your children understand what it means to be a member of your family?

DISCUSSION QUESTIONS:

Spend a few minutes as a group reacting to the following questions:

- What are your thoughts regarding Dean's statement that most teenagers think of God as either "a divine therapist" or "a cosmic butler"?
- How does your congregation talk about God?
- How does your family talk about God?
- What characteristics would you expect a "highly devoted" teenager to have? Make a list. Which of these characteristics do you see in your own student?
- How have you seen others treat Christianity as a family heirloom? How have you done that yourself?
- What God story is your family telling?
- When you read this statement from the first page of the book, do you count yourself among the "we"? "American young people are,

theoretically, fine with religious faith—but it does not concern them very much, and it is not durable enough to survive long after they graduate high school. One more thing: we're responsible."[10] How does this statement and what you've heard so far in our study together make you feel?

WORDS OF ASSURANCE

Be confident of this, "that he who began a good work in you will carry it on to completion until the day of Christ Jesus."
—Philippians 1:6 (NIV)

Lesson Two
FAITH TOOLS

CONVERSATION STARTERS:

You'd never plant a tree on a Saturday, and then expect it to bear fruit on the following Sunday. Fruit takes time to grow. Trees need care and cultivation. In the same way, faith that bears fruit doesn't just happen. Our families need opportunities to cultivate their soils. They need sunlight, food, and fertilizer.

Heirlooms

A simple way to get your family talking faith is to lay out a few family heirlooms and say something like "These are objects that remind us of important moments our family has had. These items remind us of special moments and of great memories. They help create family stories which, in turn, help flesh out some of the identity of who we are as a group."

Ask:

- How is our faith like these heirlooms?"
- What heirlooms do we have that remind us of our faith? (Family Bible, crosses displayed in your home, Baptism certificates, posted scripture verses, etc.)
- Should we create some new heirlooms to remind us who we are as a Christian family? What should they be?

Stories

Sharing family stories of the faith can be an important way to connect generational faith together. Encouraging conversations about faith with older family members can be very powerful. Share your memories of your children's grandparents' or great-grandparents' faith. If you are a first generation believer, talk with your family about what legacy of faith you hope to leave for your children and future generations.

TRADITION BUILDERS

Create a Family Creed

As we seek to help our children and youth form a strong foundation of faith, a great place to start is by creating a Family Creed. A creed is a "system or statement of beliefs." It defines exactly what a group of people believe. It is deeply theological, rooted in scripture, and somewhat outlines the core doctrines to which a group adheres.

For Christian families, a creed reminds us who we are, how we will live, and what we hope for. There are two prominent creeds from the Old Testament. One you will recognize from many Christian homes is Joshua 24:15: *"As for me and my house, we will serve the Lord." NIV*

The Jewish people had a collective creed that every Jewish child knew. This creed comes from the book of Deuteronomy, and is called the Shema.

"Hear, O Israel, the Lord is our God, the Lord is One. Blessed be the name of the glory of His kingdom forever and ever. You shall love the Lord your God with all your heart, with all your soul, and with all your might. And these words which I command you today shall be upon your heart. You shall teach them thoroughly to your children, and you shall speak of them when you sit in your house and when you walk on the road, when you lie down and when you rise. You shall bind them as a sign upon your hand, and they shall be for a reminder between your eyes. And you shall write them upon the doorposts of your house and upon your gates." Deuteronomy 6:4-9, NIV

Below are some suggestions for how to go about creating a family creed. The age of your children would affect both what your creed should look like and the level of involvement of your children in developing this creed. Younger children need simple concrete ideas of who God is. Older children and youth can actively participate in the development of the creed. See the samples below for a family with small children and one for a family with youth.

HOW TO CREATE A FAMILY CREED:

Begin by guiding your family though the following steps.

1. Ask everyone to write out a few descriptive words that help them define who God is.
2. Ask each family member to write down a few of his or her most important beliefs about God and the church.

3. Ask each family member to answer the question, "What does our relationship God mean?"
4. Ask each family member to answer the question, "How do we live in the world? How should we live with each other?"
5. Invite one family member to keep track of everyone's answers. Consider writing everything down on a white board or large piece of paper.
6. Next, ask your family to look over and think about everything that has been recorded. Ask, "How can we write out everything we've just said is important to us?

Encourage family members to work together to write out your family creed. When you're done, read it together as a family. Post it in a prominent place in your home, and revisit it regularly. Rewrite it as necessary as your children and your understandings grow.

SAMPLE CREED FOR A FAMILY WITH SMALL CHILDREN:

Young children are concrete thinkers and need direction for how to form a creed. This sample creed is a fun bedtime ritual for the family to do together. Children can memorize the responses.

Leader: How big is God?
Family: Big enough to hold the whole world in his hand, and small enough to live in my heart.
Leader: How do we know God loves us?
Family: Because Jesus died for us.
Leader: What is a family?
Family: People who love and care for each other.
Leader: Who are the Smiths?
Family: A family who loves each other and serves God and our neighbor!

SAMPLE CREED FOR A FAMILY WITH YOUTH:

As youth approach sixth and seventh grades, they need less direction for their concrete thinking, and are beginning to own and form their own beliefs. Developing a family creed with their help will continue to grow their faith. This creed is an example of a statement of belief that's appropriate for young teenagers.

"We believe in a loving God who gave everything to have a relationship with us, including Jesus Christ his son. Therefore with humble hearts, we gratefully serve God by living in harmony with each other and using our gifts to allow others to experience the love of Christ."

ADDITIONAL TRADITION BUILDER:

As a family, investigate historical Christian creeds and statements of faith. Take time to learn some of them. Ask questions about what they mean. You can find some of the historic creeds by doing a Wikipedia search or visiting EarlyChristianWritings.com. Also, most church hymnals have creeds printed in the back. Be sure to investigate your denominational or church's faith statements, which you should be able to find online.

DISORIENTING DILEMMAS

Jesus often presented people with disorienting dilemmas. We can use these in our families to further create deep faith development in our children. We can use Jesus' examples to introduce our family to the concept of disorienting dilemmas.

To begin this disorienting dilemma, choose one of the passages below:

- Mark 10:17-31
- Mark 4:35-41

Gather your family together and read the passage out loud. Then, read the passage again, and ask each family member to choose one perspective from the story and share how that person might feel, or how he or she might view this situation. Continue until you've shared all of the perspectives in the passage. When you're finished, answer these questions together:

- How was each person in the story challenged?
- What was Jesus trying to do? How did that impact everyone else?
- How does this scripture challenge us today?

Then if your children are ready, look for ways to stretch your conversation into dilemmas that are going on in the world today. Choose a dilemma from the following list:

- Christian and Muslim relations
- Christmas versus Holiday celebrations
- Religious wars
- Bullying
- Consumerism
- Death

By connecting faith to the dilemmas in their life and the world, youth actualize their faith and grow. Look for ways to engage youth in questions that invite a response, such as, "How should we (as Christians) respond to …"

EXPERIENCING TOGETHER

Stretching Experiences

As you seek to establish a baseline foundation of faith with your teenagers, having common experiences with your youth can provide opportunity for conversation and growth. Here are a few suggestions for some things you can do:

- Attend a church of another denomination. Talk about your experience at that church both in worship and how you felt as visitors.
- Attend a Catholic church if you are a protestant and a protestant church if you are a Catholic. Discuss the differences with your student.
- Attend an Episcopal church and talk about their love for the Lord's Supper.
- Go on a mission trip or youth retreat as a sponsor. Talk about what *you* learned and see if they'll share with you.
- Go to the hospital or visit friends who have a baby. Talk about how you felt when your child was a baby and your hopes, fears, and dreams for him or her.

Lesson Three
PASSING ON THE FAITH

Most religious teens in the United States appear to engage in few religious practices. But even basic practices like regular Bible reading and personal prayer seem clearly associated with stronger and deeper faith commitment among youth.[1]

—Christian Smith with Melinda Denton

SETTING THE STAGE:

In this lesson we will explore how we pass on the faith to our children by translating the gospel through our lives. We'll learn that translating God's love in human form takes using every cultural tool—stories, songs, symbols, attitudes, language, practices, and patterns of life—at the gospel's disposal. This is how the faith is ferried across generations.

FROM THE STUDY:

The NSYR testifies to young people's willingness, even eagerness, to hang out with adults who support and encourage them.[2]

The data from the NSYR suggests that American churches and families that attend church do not engage young people in faith conversations. The data also suggests that when these two groups do talk about faith issues with students, they're not providing sufficient clarity for young people to be able to distinguish the faith conversation from other conversations. In other words, according to our students, the church sounds a lot like the world as we talk about issues, leaving youth without the language tools to infuse their conversations with their faith in God. What's more, the similarities between the religious outlook of teenagers and their parents indicate that youth are not the only ones in need of faith forming conversation. Many parents feel inadequate and either abandon the religious instruction of their children altogether or turn the job over to church "experts."

But faith is a way of life, not only information to be memorized. Attendance at youth groups and church education programs are important for establishing healthy social networks, religious formation, and opportunities for spiritual reflection. However, these programs are secondary elements in the transmission of faith. Passing faith on to students takes models, not theories. It takes mentoring, not programming. Faith transmission requires communities that embody the tradition in three-dimensional form and adults who can connect these traditions to daily life. God revealed God's self-giving love in human form tells us that the faith conversations make no sense apart from a community of people who thoughtfully and faithfully follow the person of Jesus Christ.[3]

DEAN'S RESPONSE:

Dean highlights the idea that God's story shapes missional imaginations, which help us recognize God's activity in Jesus Christ and in us, as Christ calls us to participate in his redemptive work in the world. Our God story tells us who God is, shapes our ability to participate in the Christian community, and provides the means for discerning our call as disciples and for claiming our hope in God's future. Learning God's story gives teenagers cultural tools that stake up young faith, improve teenagers' exposure to the Son and therefore the likelihood that their faith will mature and bear fruit. Yet hearing God's story does not guarantee that teenagers will follow Jesus. Only the Holy Spirit lights the match of faith, transforming human effort into holy fire that comes roaring into our lives at the first hint of welcome, insistent on igniting us, sharing us, and being shared.

For centuries, two strategies—telling God's story and enacting it—comprised the heart of Christian formation, or catechesis, the "handing on" of a faith tradition from one generation to the next. Churches and families can (and must) help by plunging teenagers into Christianity's peculiar God story, and by inviting young people to take part in practices that embody it.[4]

LOOKING AT SCRIPTURE: 2 KINGS 18:26-36

Spend some time reading this passage together. If time allows look at the entire story told in chapters 18 and 19. As you read, keep the historical context of this passage in mind. This scripture serves as a model of community that converses with the broader culture, but also refuses to give in to the dominant culture's demands. Here is the story:

The Assyrians have surrounded Jerusalem, and now all attention is on-the-wall of Jerusalem that stands between the Jews and the culture that seems destined to overwhelm them. The Assyrian negotiator stands at the wall, taunting Yahweh and shouting conditions for surrender. Israel responds with a tactical move of its own. While negotiations on-the-wall with the Assyrians are being conducted in Aramaic (the official imperial language of those who dismiss Yahweh), Israel's leaders were immersed in a behind-the-wall conversation in Hebrew, the language of Judah, where Yahweh is addressed. Here is the conversation between the Assyrian leader and the Jewish field commander from 2 Kings 18:26-28

"Then Eliakim son of Hikiah, and Shebna and Joah said to the field commander, *'Please speak to your servants in Aramaic, since we understand it. Don't speak to us in Hebrew in the hearing of the people on the wall.' But the commander replied, 'Was it only to your master and you that my master sent me to say these things, and not to the people sitting on the wall – who like you, will have to eat their own excrement and drink their own urine?'*

*Then the commander stood and called out in Hebrew, 'Hear the word of the great king, the king of Assyria! This is what the kings says: Do not let Hezekiah deceive you. He cannot deliver you from my ha*nd. Do not let Hezekiah persuade you to trust in the LORD when he says, 'The LORD will surely deliver us ...'"

The behind-the-wall conversation turns out to be pivotal. Within their own community, the people of Judah speak and grieve openly in Hebrew, the intimate language of family and friendship, of worship and prayer. Speaking Hebrew behind-the-wall, the people of Judah recount stories of God's faithfulness to them, remembering that their salvation is in Yahweh's hands. Behind-the-wall, the people of Judah remember who they are—a people whom Yahweh has promised to save, whom Yahweh has called to be a blessing to all nations. These behind-the-wall conversations are decisive for what happens on-the-wall. Remembering God's faithfulness, Israel's leaders enter the on-the-wall conversation with different assumptions about the world from those of the empire—which allows them to negotiate on-the-wall, using the language of the realm, emboldened by an alternative vision of their future. Without the behind-the-wall conversation, "the language of the Empire prevails."[5]

When you're done reading the passage, reflect on these questions:

- Why are "behind-the-wall" conversations so pivotal to Israel's defense?
- What is the significance of the behind-the-wall language happening in Hebrew? Why is that important?
- How are "behind-the-wall" conversations important to your relationship to your student?

EXPLORING OUR RESPONSE:

The significance of both "behind-the-wall" and "on-the-wall" conversations is important to note. We might think that behind-the-wall conversations are the most important, because they're formational and delve into deep spiritual issues. However, think of them like this: robust behind-the-wall conversations with our students about life and faith prepare them for on-the-wall conversations about life and faith while they are "in the world," interacting with their peers.

BEHIND-THE-WALL CONVERSATIONS

In our scripture, the conversation on-the-wall shouts conditions for acceptance, but the discussion behind-the-wall refuses to give up. Behind-the-wall conversations supply youth with the tools—metaphors, stories, songs, and creeds—necessary to resist the world's views. Without transformative, imaginative, religious language, youth have only the world's conversations to describe the world. These worldly conversations present a view where Jesus does not make a difference. In a world without a loving God, Moralistic Therapeutic Deism makes perfect sense.

Dean notes: "The issue is not whether young people can read the Bible (they can). The real issue is…well, really, why would they want to? What have they seen in the church that would suggest that the Bible is a source of power and wonder? When have they seen their parents derive life and joy from reading scripture? 'We have been duped into thinking that the issue is Bible drills instead of instilling a love of reading the Bible,' Anne Florence claims. 'We have been scared into sharing information about the text instead of our passion for it.'"[6]

DISCUSSION QUESTIONS:

- What behind-the-wall conversations have taken place at your home?
- What are some things you do or can do to get your family talking about God? About the Bible? About essential elements of your faith?

- How is prayer modeled for your youth? How is your church teaching youth to pray?
- Where do your youth encounter people passionate about the word of God? At church? At home?
- Do your students have opportunities to interact with adults who are struggling with their faith?

ON-THE-WALL CONVERSATIONS:

On-the-wall conversations are conversations that our children have every day. They happen at school, at soccer practice, when they turn on the TV or Internet, when they go to the movies, etc. The importance of our behind-the-wall conversations is to prepare our children to engage in on-the-wall conversations without losing their faith! But as Dean points out, the best way for our children youth to learn on-the-wall techniques is to watch adults engage in those conversations.

DISCUSSION QUESTIONS:

- Where do your children have the opportunity to watch you or other adults engage in on-the-wall conversations?
- How have you seen other parents model on-the-wall conversations at home?
- What are the on-the-wall conversations taking place in your home? Which ones are the most challenging?

WORDS OF ASSURANCE

"Everything you need for your children's faith formation, God had already given you. Awakening faith does not depend on how hard we press young people to love God, but on how much we show them that we do." [7] —Dean

Lesson Three
FAITH TOOLS

It's important to remember that on–the-wall and behind-the-wall conversations are for one single purpose: so that the language of the empire does not prevail in the lives of our students. Faith conversations are the explicit and implicit curriculum in the lives of people of faith. We talk with our students about our beliefs, and as we do that, they are taught correct theology and doctrine. The more we chat about our beliefs, the more their beliefs are fleshed out in their lives. And the more that happens, the firmer their foundation will be.

CONVERSATION STARTERS:

Behind-the-Wall

There's nothing special about starting a behind-the-wall conversation with your student. These conversation starters below are designed to get your "behind-the-wall" conversation started with your student. You can begin with a question or by sharing something and then inviting youth to respond.

- What is your favorite scripture? Share your favorite scripture and why you love it.
- Is there something for which I can be praying for you this week? Share one of your prayer concerns or how prayer has impacted your life this week.
- What did you learn from the sermon? Was there anything you disagreed with? Share something you learned or talk about something you disagreed with in the sermon. Ask their opinion.
- What do you think is God's will for us? Is that different from what we want for ourselves? Share what you have learned about God's will from your own experiences.

On-the-Wall

On-the-wall conversations are usually best started with the person modeling sharing first. Here are some on-the-wall conversation starters you can try with your student:

- Share your experience of trying to live as a Christian in middle school, high school, or college. Then ask, "How difficult is it for you to be a Christian at school?"
- Share your experiences of parties and how you believe Christians should respond to drinking, smoking, making out, or sex. Then ask, "How do you respond when you go to a party where people are drinking, smoking, or hooking up?"
- Share your fears with your student. Then ask, "What are you most afraid of?"
- Share with her something you are trying to make a decision about related to the family, a sibling, or work. Then, ask her to share her opinion about the big decisions you're facing.
- Bring up something you have seen on the news that has faith implications like abortion, war, justice issues, death penalty, hunger, etc. Then, invite him to share what he thinks about these topics.

TRADITION BUILDERS:

Prayer Rituals

Prayer rituals are one of the most important practices a family can participate in. They engage children in communication with God, instruct them in modes of prayer, and teach them to foster an ongoing conversation with God. Family prayer rituals should grow deeper as children's faith matures. If all we ever model for our children is how to be thankful for our food, then we have not given them an essential tool for living.

You can strengthen your family's prayer time by creating rituals. Here are a few ideas:

- Create a non-negotiable family prayer time. Set one morning or evening every week for your family to pray together. Prayer times can be simple; they don't have to be overly planned.
- When you pray broaden your prayers to include concerns of the world, for our country, for our community, for our church, for our family, and for us.
- Look for ways and opportunities to let your children participate in family prayers by inviting them to lead or, consider opening up parts of the prayer time for everyone to participate.

- Take prayer concerns before the prayer. You might be surprised what they share. Model prayers that help children and youth move beyond the family cat to include our world, country, community, and church.
- Create a family prayer journal. Keep a notebook where you record the prayer concerns of your family. Reference previous prayers and how the situation has improved or worsened throughout the week.
- Consider using the historical prayers of the church or prayers from devotional books. You might investigate resources like the *Book of Uncommon Prayer*[8].

Family Bible Study

This may sound simplistic, but if we want our young people to love the Bible, then we must love it too. Start a family Bible study that meets once a week. You can do it during a meal. Look at the scriptures, raise questions, and search for answers together. Don't try to be the expert, and don't feel like you have to answer every question. Students actually value learning with their parents.

There are dozens of Bible study guides available online. Do an internet search for possible study helps. If you come up short, consider starting with www.biblestudytools.net or www.bible.org to get you started. As you study, be sure and explore the text and ask questions.

Texting Ministry to Your Child

If you have small children, start a tradition of putting a short note with a scripture on it in their lunchbox or book bag to remind them who they are when they are in the world.

If your teenagers have cell phones, you have easy access into their brains. Send your youth a text every day with a short scripture verse in it to remind them that God loves them and you do, too.

DISORIENTING DILEMMAS

Take your family to a center where disenfranchised people come for food, clothing or shelter, like a food pantry or a homeless shelter. Call the center in advance and set up a time when your family can tour, and then spend several hours helping out. Serve food, fold clothes, clean the facilities. Do whatever work you can do to give your children a feel for the kind of work that's being done at the facility.

Make sure you plan for interaction with the people who use the services of the location where you're serving. Consider eating with them, or interviewing them, or possibly working alongside them in the shelter. As they interact with these people, encourage your kids to chat with them, asking them questions about their lives and where they have come from.

At the end of the day, sit down with your family and invite everyone to share the experiences they had, including the conversations they had with those who live and work there. Use this interaction to ask your student disorienting questions about their experiences.

EXPERIENCING TOGETHER

Intentional Faith Passing

On-the-wall and behind-the-wall conversations often happen as a result of crises, or moments where students are disoriented. You can create faith experiences simply by putting your students into situations where their pursuits of God are challenged in new ways. Here are a few different ideas (of varying degrees of difficulty) that will help put your child in a place where she will talk about her faith and, as a result, engage in healthy faith conversations.

- Commit to doing a once-a-week spiritual practice together.
- Fast one meal a week and as you do, gather together and discuss how it felt to go without food. Then, discuss why you're not eating, and what fasting means.
- Memorize one scripture passage a week and say it to each other at meal times. Discuss what it means to "hide God's word in our hearts," and how remembering scripture shapes who they are.
- Commit to doing fifteen minutes of Lectio Divina together twice a week. After each Lectio session, discuss what you heard the Holy Spirit saying to you, and what you need to do as a result of what you heard.
- Go on a family retreat. You don't need to go to an expensive vacation spot. Spend a few hours at a friend's house, or rent a hotel room for one night. While you're there, spend time reading scripture and praying as a family. Be sure to include worship as part of the family retreat. While you're there experiencing this event together, engage your student in faith conversations.
- Take your family on a mission trip, or, sign up as an adult on the next youth mission trip. Choose a safe place to take your family. Engage in work together, and use the work you do to spur your family into faith conversations.

Lesson Four
TESTIFY: BY WORD AND ACTION

*If I have achieved anything in my life, it has been
because I have not been embarrassed to talk about God.*[1]

—Dorothy Day

SETTING THE STAGE:

In this lesson we will be challenged to explore how we immerse and engage
our young people in conversations about our faith. Teenagers who have trouble articulating what they believe about God also seem to have trouble forging
a significant connection to God—and youth who do not have a language for
Christ are unlikely to imagine an identity in Christ.[2]

FROM THE STUDY:

One of the major findings of the NSYR is that youth are incredibly inarticulate about faith. Young people who can talk about almost anything else shut
down when asked about their faith. Smith and Denton note that, "The language, and therefore experience, of Trinity, holiness, sin, grace, justification,
sanctification, church, Eucharist, and heaven and hell appear, among most
Christian teenagers in the United States at the very least, to be supplanted by
the language of happiness, niceness, and an earned heavenly reward."[3]

Apart from Mormons and some conservative Protestants, the NSYR suggests that most American teenagers have enormous difficulty putting religious
faith into words.[4] African American communities are also an exception to
this rule, because religious language is a part of the cultural vernacular of
these communities, which allows teenagers to hear it spoken.[5]

DEAN'S RESPONSE:

The exceptions to those who were inarticulate were highly devoted teenagers, who *could* talk about what they believed, and who *did* share stories about religion's impact on their lives—stories in which God had urgency and was not merely a distant bystander.[6]

We do know that giving young people opportunities to talk about faith in families and congregations is positively correlated with holding religious conviction that they can articulate, critically examine, and confess.[7]

A likely explanation of the absence of theological vocabularies in teenagers is simply the absence of robust theological conversation in the environments teenagers inhabit—certainly the worlds of the media and public education, but also the worlds of families and congregations. Since youth do not hear a language of faith, they do not speak one. Without a narrative to give such chatter coherence and meaning, teenagers are left to cobble together a patchwork religious system, borrowed, not from deeply anchored faith traditions or a growing recognition of God's activity in the world, but from appealing parts of a number of myths Americans live by.[8]

If Jesus does not get talked about, he soon fades from teenagers' awareness, and therefore vanishes from their structures of meaning.[9]

LOOKING AT SCRIPTURE: ACTS 1:8; 2 TIMOTHY 1:8

Dean states, "We cannot keep quiet about someone who loves us this much."[10]. We talk about things we love, but we must ask ourselves, does our love for Christ show up in conversations with our students? Do we talk about these things in our homes?

"Testify" and "witness" are words that can stir up feelings of rivals and evangelists. However, we are called to testify and to witness to God's love in the world. Read the following scriptures and share with someone or the group what feelings they evoke in you.

"But you will receive power when the Holy Spirit comes on you; and you will be my **witness**es in Jerusalem, and in all Judea and Samaria, and to the ends of the earth." Acts 1:8 NIV

"So do not be ashamed to **testify** about our Lord…" 2 Timothy 1:8 NIV

After a short time of reflection, discuss these questions as a group:

- What does it mean to "testify about our Lord" in our homes? What does this look like?

- In the Acts passage, how are "power" and "witness" connected? Why do you think Jesus connects them together? What are the implications of this connection in your home?
- Discuss the last "faith conversation" you had with your student. What was the conversation about? How did it begin?

EXPLORING OUR RESPONSE:

As we explored in our last session, behind-the-wall conversations are important for establishing our Christian identity in the larger culture. Testimony plays a part in both behind-the-wall and on-the-wall conversations.

If learning to speak "Christian" is similar to learning any language, then the first thing that must happen is for children and youth to be immersed in a family and community that speaks "Christian." Testimony becomes an important part of how we teach young people both at home and in our churches. Testimony is to give witness—"to see and to tell."[11]

There are two ways we can help our youth experience testimony: *eavesdropping* and *faith immersions*.

EAVESDROPPING

Eavesdropping is one of the important components of learning to speak Christian, as teenagers learn to articulate faith by hearing adults articulate theirs.[12] Testimony tells about a time when, by the sheer force of grace, God's story and our story collided.[13]

Eavesdropping is an opportunity to "see and to tell" our students about what God has and is doing in our lives. It's one of our responsibilities as we endeavor to pass on the faith. Your story is made up of a bunch of little stories; learn to tell the little ones and your children will experience the big one. Our responsibility as parents is to create "eavesdropping moments" where we share our faith publicly in the presence of our student. These can be moments of public presentation (a testimony at church), moments with friends (praying with them, singing together, saying grace before a meal), or private family moments (praying together before bedtime, reading and discussing a scripture together). In these eavesdropping moments, we are striving to demonstrate to our students both our personal theology and our passion for knowing Christ.

DISCUSSION QUESTIONS:

- What adults would you like for your children to have the opportunity to eavesdrop on?
- What positive and negative connotations come to mind when you hear the word "testimony"?
- How have you testified about God's love to your family?
- How could testimony become a part of your family's tradition or life?
- Spend a few minutes together and practice testifying. Share one moment of God's grace in your life. How might you share that moment with your entire family?

FAITH IMMERSIONS

Faith immersions are exactly what they sound like. Young people participate in intense experiences that provide opportunity to explore faith. Camps, mission trips, and youth group retreats are all examples of faith immersions.

These faith immersions are similar to a youth participating in language immersions (e.g., an English-speaking student who desires to learn French or Spanish). Just as a language immersion exposes youth to conversational French or Spanish and forces them to join in the conversation, faith immersions expose youth to testimony and Christ-talk and invite them to join in.

Parents have an important role to play related to faith immersions. They can provide guidance and help prepare our children for their experiences. We also should help our children debrief these experiences afterwards. We can create an environment where they can testify to us about how they experienced God.

DISCUSSION QUESTIONS:

- What faith immersions had a significant impact on you as a youth?
- What faith immersions are available at your church?
- What questions have you asked that prompted a response when they returned from a faith immersion?

WORD OF ASSURANCE

"Your story is about hope, doubt, failure, and triumph. It's about standing up for justice, showing mercy, and living for God."[14] —Tony Campolo

Lesson Four
FAITH TOOLS

"Testifying" doesn't have to be about standing at a microphone and giving your testimony. You don't have to walk up to a stranger and start an evangelism conversation to testify, either. Testifying is simply taking the opportunity to share the goodness of God in your life. When we engage in "testifying moments" with our students, we're helping them see the power of remembering God's actions in our lives.

CONVERSATION STARTERS:

Family Circle

To get these kind of conversations started with your students, try this: write each of the questions below on an index card and place the cards in the center of your family circle. Ask each family member to pick up one card, offer an answer to that question, then open the discussion to allow each family member to offer his or her answer. As family members share their answers, unpack some of the theological ideas you're hearing.

- Tell your salvation story. Be bold: tell the details you might find mundane or even a bit scary.
- Share two significant experiences in your faith journey.
- Name three people who have been saints in your life. Say *why* they have been important in your journey. Share what you learned from them.
- Share significant principles you learned through experiences or study that grew your understanding of God, Jesus, and the Holy Spirit.

TRADITION BUILDER:

God Sightings

God is present and at work in our lives and the world every second, yet we are rarely aware of God's presence. One simple tradition that you can start as a family is to create a daily habit of sharing "God sightings."

Start the tradition of sharing moments when each of you has "seen God" as you've walked along in life. This sharing can happen at breakfast, before you go to bed, or at any other opportune time when the entire family is together. Use this tradition to build stronger God talk and provide space for testimony in your home.

Use these questions to help guide your sharing:

- Where did you see God at work in the world or in others today?
- How did you experience God in your life today?
- What did you do with God's help today?

DISORIENTING DILEMMAS

Share Your Story

Are you comfortable sharing your faith with others? Are your children? Consider creating a disorienting dilemma with you students through *practice*. You don't have to preach on the corner. You can fully engage others in conversation on the subway, at a restaurant, or at the soccer game. Look for opportunities to share some aspect of your faith.

This disorienting dilemma is easy to set up. Take your family to a place where people gather (a coffee shop, restaurant or park) and engage others in simple, everyday conversations. Encourage your students to drop their beliefs and worldview into the conversation they're having. If you need a medium to get the conversation going, pass out water bottles or peanut butter and jelly sandwiches to the homeless.

WORTH DYING FOR?

We are fortunate to live in a free country where we practice our religious beliefs freely. However, there are nations around the world where Christianity is against the law. The church has been built on the blood of the martyrs—people willing to die for Christ. Consider creating a disorienting dilemma through studying the martyrs.

Visit www.voiceofthemartyrs.com, or pick up *Jesus Freaks* or *Fox's Book of Martyrs* and read several stories to your family. After you've read their stories, talk openly with your youth about whether each of you would be willing to die for your faith.

Now investigate ways that your family might respond to persecution around the world. You might pray for persecuted Christians, or do some online investigation into organizations that take the Gospel into dangerous places and how you can support those people.

EXPERIENCING TOGETHER

An incredible way to engage your student in faith conversations is to take everyone on a family pilgrimage. A pilgrimage is simply a religious journey. Most pilgrimages that we hear about are long trips to the Holy Land, but you can create short pilgrimages near your home. You could pilgrimage by going to:

- A local monastery and experiencing the worship and community of the monks. A visit to their website will have information about a day visit or short retreats.
- A Catholic church that has a labyrinth or the Stations of the Cross and experience them together.
- A Cathedral and investigate the symbols, altars, and stained glass together as a family.
- Your denomination's nearby camps or other Christian camps that will likely have special places of worship as well recreational things you can do as a family.
- A significant place on your faith journey where you can share how you experienced God in that place.

Lesson Five
TRANSFORMATION THROUGH DISORIENTATION

Deep down, I'm afraid of this return to luxury. Or perhaps afraid is not the right word—more like reluctant, or wary. I don't want to slip into my pre-Mexico self like a hermit crab returning to an abandoned shell, and I know how easy it could be.[1]

—Junior High Youth Gabrielle Hovendon
after Mexico Mission Trip

SETTING THE STAGE:

This lesson will challenge us to explore how to create arenas where students can explore their faith. Instead of creating comfort zones for teenagers to practice their faith, we should create disorienting dilemmas and reflective practices that allow the Holy Spirit to move and create growth.

FROM THE STUDY:

The National Study of Youth and Religion defined spiritual experience operationally (and narrowly) as a commitment to live one's life for God, an experience of powerful worship, an answered prayer or sense of divine guidance, or the experience or witnessing of a miracle. Only Jewish and nonreligious teenagers in the study were very unlikely to have "made a personal commitment to live life for God," and more than one in five nonreligious teenagers said they had witnessed "a miracle from God." Seventy-five percent of Mormon and conservative Protestant teenagers, and almost as many mainline Protestant youth, say they have worshipped in moving and powerful ways (only Catholic teenagers had trouble thinking of a meaningful experience of worship). More than half of Christian teenagers interviewed said that they had witnessed a divine miracle, that God answered their prayers, or gave them specific guidance. All told, four out of five American teenagers reported having had a religious experience—and 40 percent named three or more.[2]

DEAN'S RESPONSE:

Teaching toward transformation typically involves four distinct moments:

1. A disorienting dilemma.
2. Critical self-reflection on our prior assumptions.
3. Discourse that puts into words the insights derived from our critical reflection.
4. Action.[3]

When a student encounters disorienting dilemmas, old ideas fall apart, and… "she stands on unfamiliar ground, unguarded against new ideas, new relationships, new roles, and new sources of hope. Her defenses melt, making her pliable to Holy Spirit's prompting to think about God, herself, and others in new ways."[4]

The uncertainty of the new situation launches a period of self-reflection and scanning for new options as we examine our prior assumptions, figure out what tools are missing or no longer operable, and look for new resources that can resolve the dissonance. Transformative learning does not just yield new information; it incites a paradigm shift.[5]

LOOKING AT SCRIPTURE: 1 SAMUEL 1:10-11; 26-27

In the passage for this lesson, Hannah encounters a disorienting dilemma in her life—she has not born a son. As you read, think about how Hannah giving her son to the Lord creates a disorienting dilemma for all parents. Spend some time exploring this passage together.

"In her deep anguish Hannah prayed to the LORD, weeping bitterly. And she made a vow, saying, "LORD Almighty, if you will only look on your servant's misery and remember me, and not forget your servant but give her a son, then I will give him to the LORD for all the days of his life, and no razor will ever be used on his head."

"Pardon me, my lord. As surely as you live, I am the woman who stood here beside you praying to the LORD. I prayed for this child, and the LORD has

granted me what I asked of him. So now I give him to the LORD. For his whole life he will be given over to the LORD." And he worshipped the LORD there."

Take several minutes to discuss these questions with another adult in the group:

- How might your desires for your children be in line with God's desires for your children?
- Are you called to give your children to the Lord?
- Is there anything that God might call your son or daughter to do that you would be uncomfortable with? Doctor to children in Africa? Preacher? Missionary?

Pray with each other that you would have the courage to give your children to the Lord.

EXPLORING OUR RESPONSE

Disorienting dilemmas and faithful interaction are two important components to creating environments where students can explore their faith. Let's explore each of these elements further.

DISORIENTING DILEMMAS

We want to help young people and ourselves experience what medieval theologians called *detachment*. Detachment is simply stepping out of our comfortable surroundings and regular way of life so that we can focus all our attention on Jesus Christ. Disorienting dilemmas free us to see new ideas, they change how we see the world, others, and our self. *We are most open to divine reconstruction when we lose our balance, when the Legos® of our carefully constructed selves fall apart so that God can rebuild us in new ways.*[6]

Work together as a group to make a list of disorienting faith dilemmas. If you need help getting started, refer to the passage. Talk about how death, birth, accidents, moves, mission trips, broken relationships, etc. create disorienting dilemmas and affect people's understanding of God.

DISCUSSION QUESTIONS:

Spend several minutes discussing these questions as a group.

- When have you experienced disorienting dilemmas in your life?

- How did that dilemma change your understanding of the world? God? Yourself?
- What dilemmas has your family faced?
- As a parent have you sought to create a safe place for faith exploration or sought to create detachment where youth encounter disorientation?

FAITHFUL REFLECTION

Spiritual experiences are meaningless without reflection that leads to new understandings and knowledge. Likewise, spiritual knowledge is not life transforming without experiences to turn that knowledge into faith. We want to help young people process things. We want them to take ownership of their faith as they fully embrace new insights and understandings. When a spiritual experience and faithful reflection come together, they create "a-ha" moments for teenagers that rewire their understanding of God.

DISCUSSION QUESTIONS:

Spend several minutes discussing these questions as a group.

- How do you promote spiritual reflection in your home? When do you talk about spiritual experiences like the ones you listed above?
- How have you prepared your children for experiences that might have at camp, on a mission trip, or a sacrament at church? How can you help them process these experiences when they return?
- When you have had a spiritual experience, what has helped you process and talk about it? What are some ways to help your children put words to theirs?

WORD OF ASSURANCE

In the midst of positive and negative disorienting dilemmas, remember that the Holy Spirit is at work and that only God can bring about changed lives. We are instruments. Trips and events are opportunities for God to work, but it's God who does the work in our souls.

Lesson Five
FAITH TOOLS

CONVERSATION STARTERS:

Your family is searching for transformation, though they might not phrase it like that. They might say, "I wish we did more things together" or they might ask, "Why don't we ever pray together?" When our kids ask those kinds of questions, they're looking to us to create moments of transformation, opportunities to connect the family together, and grow closer to God. Use the following questions to get your kids talking about the transformation that's happening inside them.

- What do you believe are your spiritual gifts?
- Why do you think God created you and put you in this family?
- What do you believe God wants you to do with your life?
- How might you use your gifts to share God's love?
- Name someone you look up to who serves God with his or her life. Why do you look up to him or her?
- What do you think God wants you to study in college? What makes you feel that way?

TRADITION BUILDER

Spiritual Letters

As our children get older, our conversations with them change. We use different language with younger children, and we discuss more abstract concepts with our older teens. Connecting with our kids is essential, but it's not always easy.

Writing letters to our children is an effective way to share deep ideas with them in a way that isn't awkward. Look for moments when you see God working in your student, and then write them a letter about what you're seeing. Birthdays, baptismal birthday, and events like heading off to camp or a mission trip are all good opportunities to write letter.

As you write your teen a letter, consider these guiding ideas.

- How have you seen her grow?
- What gifts, skills, and talents have you seen him use for God?
- How has she made you proud?
- Where did you see God at work in his life?
- What are your hopes for her future?
- What are your prayers for him?
- What do you hope and pray for her at camp, on the mission trip, or as she begins the next phase of her spiritual journey?

DISORIENTING DILEMMAS

Others

"Others" are people not like you. They may look different, speak different, be in a different socio-economic status, or of a different nationality. As a family, talk about the people who are "others" to you in your community.

Now talk about the "others" your family is interacting with. How might these interactions challenge and grow your understanding of who you are and who God is through those people?

Make a commitment as a family to enter into a relationship that creates space for God to introduce you to a bigger world than you currently know. Consider these ways to interact with those you don't normally talk to:

- Eat in a different part of town and engage those around you in conversation.
- Participate on a community project and help serve different neighborhoods in your city.
- Begin a relationship with a family on your street that no one talks to.

If you have younger children, discuss the importance of allowing your children to know "others" and look for age appropriate ways to introduce them to a larger world.

EXPERIENCING TOGETHER

Living into the Mission of God

Dean points out that mission is not a trip. Participating in God's active work in the world is essential for fostering an understanding of God's call in our lives. By serving others, we open ourselves up to the Holy Spirit, and we hear God's voice urging us toward our callings. Engaging our young people in the work of God is essential in their formation into God's people.

Moving your family into this place involves a few simple steps.

First, get the family together and spend a few minutes in individual silent prayer. Ask God how he wants your family to serve him this year, and then instruct members to listen for God's voice or leading.

Second, invite each person to share what he or she heard. Encourage family members to remain silent if they don't feel God spoke to them. Gather the responses and see how they fit together.

Third, look over the list and decide how you will serve God this year. Invite family members to share their ideas based on the list you've created.

Fourth, decide how you will implement these service ideas. Consider starting with once a month if you're a busy family.

Fifth, schedule check-up times. Agree that you will meet together after your first planned service and debrief about what you've just experienced, and commit to plan your next service at that meeting.

Sixth, ask the youngest family member to close in prayer, asking God to be glorified in your family service times.

Lesson Six
HOPE FOR TOMORROW

Make no small plans. They have no magic to stir humanity's blood and probably themselves will not be realized. Make big plans; aim high in hope and work... Remember that our sons and daughters are going to do things that will stagger us. Let your watchword be order and your beacon, beauty. Think big.[1]

—Daniel Burnham

SETTING THE STAGE:

Today's lesson will challenge us to explore the importance of hope in establishing faith in young people.

Young people often struggle with doubt. Doubt and hope are closely related. What separates hope from doubt is hope's ability to stand in the known and look expectantly into the unknown. Since Christians believe that God is responsible for the future and that Jesus Christ has already redeemed it, this expectancy fills us with joy instead of dread. We have hope for our young people—not because we are faithful, but because God is.[2]

FROM THE STUDY:

As we discovered early in the study, Dean developed her response by looking at what the NSYR, supported by the Exemplary Youth Ministry study, learned about highly devoted teens. Highly devoted congregations have youth and adults who understand they are an active part in the Christian God-story.

Consequential faith is faith that matters. What we have learned from faith communities that consistently demonstrate consequential faith is:

1. Religious formation is not an accident.

2. The cultural tools associated with consequential faith are available to every Christian faith community.
3. Consequential faith has risks. The love of Christ is love that is worth dying for.
4. We must reclaim our call to follow Christ into the world.

These four findings provide hope for our churches and our families. If we are intentional in our faith development with young people, consequential faith can happen. However, we must ask ourselves why we do not find more faith communities and families developing consequential faith in young people. Dean's response can help us understand.

DEAN'S RESPONSE:

American culture's fascination with success is ingrained in teenagers who have been taught that the church is great as long as they get something out of it (social acceptance or status, help when you are in trouble, that it will look good on your college résumé). Youth and parents are correct if they think that Moralistic Therapeutic Deism will outfit them better for success in American society than Christianity will.[3]

Moralistic Therapeutic Deism sets our sights on ourselves. True Christians set their hopes on Jesus Christ. Our faith tells us that we are not here for ourselves.[4]

Young people are looking to us for meaning and hope. We find meaning and hope in our call to participate in God's redemptive plan through Jesus Christ. They can see it in adults who are faithfully empowered by the Holy Spirit who follow Christ into the world. When we "get it right, Christian discipleship means following a God who loved us enough to die for us, and who calls us to love others just as deeply."[5]

LOOKING AT SCRIPTURE: MATTHEW 19:16-22

Read this scripture as a group. Notice that the young Jew in this scripture is a candidate for one of Moralistic Therapeutic Deism's common traits. His question is about what he can get out of religion. Dean would remind you that young people can identify with the rich young man's eagerness to please.

Just then a man came up to Jesus and asked, "Teacher, what good thing must I do to get eternal life?" "Why do you ask me about what is good?" Jesus replied. "There is only One who is good. If you want to enter life, keep the commandments."

"Which ones?" he inquired. Jesus replied, "'You shall not murder, you shall not commit adultery, you shall not steal, you shall not give false testimony, honor your father and mother,' and 'love your neighbor as yourself.'"

"All these I have kept," the young man said. "What do I still lack?"

Jesus answered, "If you want to be perfect, go, sell your possessions and give to the poor, and you will have treasure in heaven. Then come, follow me."

When the young man heard this, he went away sad, because he had great wealth.

This scripture points out one of the great tensions of Moralistic Therapeutic Deism—our selfish desires in contrast with giving our life away for Christ. Jesus clearly points out that following the law is not about being good. Following Jesus is about giving up our will for God's will. Jesus' words, while hard for the young man, clearly point him in the direction of hope. The way of hope is paved with surrender. His way is counter to the way of the world, and it involves risk. Faith formation does not happen by accident. It is born out of intentional decisions to follow Christ despite the cost or consequences.

EXPLORING OUR RESPONSE:

Dean tells a story about Lizzie a 14-year-old who she says, "believes that her life has a purpose, and a divinely created one at that. This purposefulness gives her hope; she believes God will use her for something good—"to change the world," as she puts it—and in doing so she is certain that she is following Christ, helping to bring God's will to fruition.

A creed, a community, a call, a hope—all cast in a particular story through which Jesus confronts Lizzie at home and at school, and sends her out to love the world on his behalf.[6]

You have great hopes and dreams for your children. Have you rooted them in God's will? Your call as a parent is to share your faith, form a faith community around your child, help him hear God's call, and to help her believe and hope through the power of Christ.

DISCUSSION QUESTIONS:

Spend a few minutes as a group discussing the following questions:

- What do you dream about for your kids' lives?
- What are your hopes for your son or daughter as it relates to his or her faith?

- How do these hopes differ from your hopes for their lives?
- In our scripture, Jesus called the young man to be more than a good person. How do we call our children to live beyond the "morals"? To be more than just "good kids"?
- Have you ever felt like Lizzie? Has your child?
- What do you hope your children get out of church? Socialization? Morals? Life-altering faith?

WORD OF ASSURANCE

"We have hope for our young people—not because we are faithful, but because God is." —Kenda Creasy Dean

Lesson Six
FAITH T●●LS

The healthiest place for students to understand and engage in hope is in your home. Studies show that the more students see and experience hope, they become stronger believers out in the world. Too often, parents believe their children need more "things," when in reality, speaking words of hope provides significant faith formation. Engage your students in talking about hope. Use these activities to get that conversation started.

CONVERSATION STARTERS:

Hopes and Dreams

Rooting our students in hope is an essential step in their spiritual formation. Begin by reading Jeremiah 29:11 aloud as a family.

> *"For I know the plans I have for you declares the Lord...Plans to give you hope and a future." Jeremiah 29:11, NIV*

Next, take the time to talk with your children about their hopes and dreams by asking them the following questions:

- What do you want to invest your life in doing? What do you want to be when you get older?
- What do you think God's hopes and dreams are for you?
- Who does God want you to be?

As you ask your children these questions, remember that the heart of our study is to turn the tide of Moralistic Therapeutic Deism away from leading students into the morass of Benign Whateverism. Help reframe students' questions by remembering that it's...

- Not where do you want to go to college but where does God want you to go to college?

- Not what do you want to be when you grow up but what does God want you to do with your life?
- Not do I want to marry him or her but does God want me to marry him or her?

TRADITION BUILDERS:

Spiritual Goals or Resolutions

Many people set personal goals throughout the year or annually create New Year's resolutions (that they often don't keep). Sometimes, those goals involve someone's personal relationship with God. Having spiritual goals, benchmarks, or resolutions as a family can be a powerful way to grow in your faith. You could work as a family to decide what your collective goals should be like. Here are some examples:

- We will serve as a family at a mission once a quarter.
- We will have a weekly family devotional time
- We learn a weekly memory verse.
- We will go to church every Sunday and worship as a family.

Invite family members to set individual spiritual goals that they share with the rest of the family. Sharing the goals allows the family to hold each other accountable in God's grace as you seek to accomplish the goals. At one of your devotional times each month, check in and see how everyone is doing with his or her goals.

DISORIENTING DILEMMAS

Explore the Holocaust together as a family; learn about the destructive and sinful nature of the human heart. Explore the hope and faith of the Jews who lived to tell their stories of horror. Allow this historical dilemma to speak into your lives as you ponder your own faith. Here are some ways that you can explore the Holocaust:

- Visit a Holocaust museum
- Watch a movie about the Holocaust
- Read a book that tells the stories of Holocaust victims

Obviously, this dilemma is for older youth. Younger children can explore the hope that exists in death through our faith in Christ. Attending a funeral can provide the space to talk about our hope for eternity in Christ.

EXPERIENCING TOGETHER

Looking for Signs of Hope

Alexandar Pope said "hope springs eternal." American society struggles with hope; therefore, we must teach our children how to see signs of hope in their everyday life. Because of our faith, we can find hope anywhere.

Sometimes, we confuse hoping and wishing. When we wish for something, we cross our fingers and wait for it to happen. Hope involves belief and action. Help your children begin to look for and identify hope in the world, by looking for places where something better is coming because someone is working to make it so.

Here are some places you can look together:

- Visiting a friend after the birth of a child allows you to talk about God's great hopes for every one of God's children.
- Every year spring brings new life. Take a nature walk and look for signs of hope springing forth all around.
- Watch for rainbows after the rain.
- Talk to the leader of a non-profit agency that your family has an interest in supporting. Listen for the hope they have. These leaders embody hope as they believe that things will change.
- Practice identifying people in your community who are bringing hope to others be working and believing they are and will make a difference.
- Practice hoping instead of wishing. Someone who simply wishes they can ride a bike never will. Someone who hopes to learn to ride a bike believes that through practice an effort they can someday.

These practices will be invaluable as your children and youth begin to identify God's work everywhere.

Lesson Seven
FINAL REFLECTIONS

NOW WHAT?

Stop and consider the road you have traveled in this study:

- You have explored the results from the National Study on Youth and Religion.
- You have learned Kenda Creasy Dean's recommendations to churches and families in response to the NSYR.
- You have explored what Dean believes creates consequential faith.
- You have tried out some practical ideas and tools to use in your family to strengthen and grow faith in your children and youth.

So, the fair question we must ask ourselves is, *now what?* What have we really learned? Has this information made a difference in how we think about our families? Have the exercises, discussions and interactions reshaped how we build faith formation in the lives of our students? What will you do with what you have learned?

You are the most influential person in your child's faith. What will your next steps be as you seek to encourage your children to be faithful disciples?

Explore these questions as you evaluate what tools where the most effective for your family.

- Which conversation starters produced the best behind-the-wall conversations?
- Were you able to share your testimony with your child? How did they respond?
- Which "disorienting dilemmas" created space for growth and conversation with your youth?
- What "experiencing together" project did you do as a family that provided the greatest sense of joy for everyone?

Take time to think about each of the tools that were presented throughout the study and brainstorm how you will apply them going forward.

CONVERSATION STARTERS

Identify five faith conversations you want to have with your student:

1.

2.

3.

4.

5.

Now that you've identified these conversations, stop and think about timing. When do you want to have these conversations? How will you frame them? Write some of your ideas below.

TRADITION BUILDERS:

Hopefully, you have had the opportunity to try one of the suggested tradition builders. It would be hard to add every tradition builder in this series to your family's life. What traditions will you put in place? Pick one or two to start with and create an action plan for how you'll get started.

1.

2.

My action plan for engaging in these tradition builders with my family is:

DISORIENTING DILEMMAS:

Life brings its own disorienting dilemmas. However, accidental dilemmas are not always faith focused. All disorienting dilemmas provide space for spiritual reflection and growth. Ask yourself what situations in your youth's life right now are creating disorienting dilemmas that you can speak into?

1.

2.

What opportunities for your family to be challenged are available through your church or community to create space reflection and growth? Which ones might your family try out next?

1.

2.

EXPERIENCING TOGETHER

What two experiences will you schedule over the next year with your children that will model and create opportunities for conversation about how Christians live out their faith?

1.

2.

You as a parent are the most influential person in your child's life. It's hard to believe they let us parent without a license. You are not a Biblical scholar (and those who are struggle to pass on the faith as well) nor do you have all the answers. However, God calls us to live faithful lives in response to God's grace. As parents, we are to bring, help, lead, and encourage our children as they join us on this incredible journey of faith. As you are now aware, this resource does not contain any magical formula for Christian discipleship; instead it offers suggestions for how your family can live life together as a part of God's family.

Find a group of families that desire these things for their children and learn from each other. Do some of the experiencing together activities together as a community. Get together with the other parents every three months to hold each other accountable and pray for each other.

My hope for you is that you will use this resource and the teachings within it to go and faithfully serve Jesus Christ with your family. Use these ideas consistently, and show your children what a person of faith looks like. The more you do that, the more they'll catch on, and eventually, they'll live out their own faith story, for the glory of Jesus Christ.

WORKS CITED

FORWARD

1. 1. See Christian Smith with Melinda Denton, *Soul Searching: The Religious and Spiritual Lives of Teenagers* (New York: Oxford), 2004.

INTRODUCTION

1. Smith, Christian and Denton, Melinda Lundquist. (2005). *Soul Searching: The Religious and Spiritual Lives of American Teenagers*. New York: Oxford University Press. pg. 171
2. Smith reports that 65 percent of teenagers believe in a God who is a "personal being involved in the lives of people." Roughly 30 percent of teenagers believe in a "spiritual force in the universe."
3. *Soul Searching*, 68.
4. *Soul Searching*, 40.
5. *Soul Searching*, 262.
6. *Soul Searching*, 218.
7. *Soul Searching*, 68.

LESSON 1

1. Dean, K. C. (2010) *Almost Christian: What the Faith of Our Teenagers is Telling the American Church*. New York: Oxford University Press. pg. 1
2. *Almost Christian*, pg. 17-18
3. *Almost Christian*, pg. 14
4. Dean, K. C. (2010) http://kendadean.com/371/moralistic-therapeutic-deism/
5. *Almost Christian*, pg. 29
6. *Almost Christian*, pg. 121

LESSON 2

1. *Almost Christian*, pg. 36
2. Almost Christian, pg. 41
3. Roland Martinson, "The Spirit and Culture of Youth Ministry: A Study of Congregations with Youth of Vital Faith" (working paper, Luther Theological Seminary, October 12, 2004), appendix A.
4. *Almost Christian*, pg. 37
5. *Almost Christian*, pg. 37
6. *Almost Christian*, pg. 70
7. *Almost Christian*, pg. 62
8. *Almost Christian*, pg. 88

LESSON 3

1. *Soul Searching*, pg. 269

2. *Soul Searching*, pg. 60
3. *Almost Christian*, pg. 117
4. *Almost Christian*, pg. 62
5. *Almost Christian*, pg. 113-114
6. *Almost Christian*, pg. 129
7. Anna Carter Florence, *Preaching as Testimony* (Louisville, KY: Westminster John Knox, 2007), 124.
8. *Almost Christian*, pg. 120
9. Case, Steven. *Book of Uncommon Prayer* (Zondervan/Youth Specialties, 2002).

LESSON 4

1. Jim Forest, "Dorothy Day," in *The Encyclopedia of American Catholic History*, ed. Michael Glazier and Thomas J. Shelley (Collegeville, MN: Liturgical Press, 1991), 414.
2. *Almost Christian*, pg. 142
3. *Soul Searching*, pg. 171
4. *Almost Christian*, pg. 132
5. *Almost Christian*, pg. 138-139
6. *Almost Christian*, pg. 135
7. *Almost Christian*, pg. 137
8. *Almost Christian*, pg. 138
9. *Almost Christian*, pg. 140
10. *Almost Christian*, pg. 141
11. *Almost Christian*, pg. 146
12. *Almost Christian*, pg. 152
13. *Almost Christian*, pg. 146
14. Campolo, Tony. *Let Me Tell You a Story: Life Lessons from Unexpected Places and Unlikely People* (Nashville, TN: Word Publishing, 2000).

LESSON 5

1. *Almost Christian*, pg. 158
2. *Soul Searching*, pg. 44-45
3. Jack Mezirow et al., *Learning as Transformation* (San Francisco: Jossey-Bass, 2000), 22.
4. *Almost Christian*, pg. 171-172
5. *Almost Christian*, pg. 175-176
6. *Almost Christian*, pg. 170

LESSON 6

1. Cited by L. Gregory Jones, "Think Big," *Christian Century* (August 23, 2005), 29. Burnham designed the 1893 Chicago World's Fair, Manhattan's Flatiron Building, and Union Station in Washington, DC.
2. *Almost Christian*, pg. 188-189
3. *Almost Christian*, pg. 191
4. *Almost Christian*, pg. 192
5. *Almost Christian*, pg. 193
6. *Almost Christian*, pg. 196

Made in the USA
Middletown, DE
19 March 2017